CARIBBEAN WRITERS SERIES

29

Jamaica Woman

CARIBBEAN WRITERS SERIES

* Available in four colour trade editions

Jamaica Woman

An Anthology of Poems

Edited by
PAMELA MORDECAI AND MERVYN MORRIS

HEINEMANN
LONDON · KINGSTON

Heinemann Educational Books Ltd.
22 Bedford Square, London WC1B 3HH
175 Mountain View Avenue, Kingston 6, Jamaica

IBADAN   NAIROBI   EDINBURGH
MELBOURNE   AUCKLAND   SINGAPORE
KUALA LUMPUR   NEW DELHI

Heinemann Educational Books Inc.
70 Court Street, Portsmouth, New Hampshire 03801, USA

Selection and arrangement
© Heinemann Educational Books (Caribbean) Ltd. 1980

First published 1980
Reprinted 1985, 1987

ISBN 0 435 98600 7

Printed in Great Britain by
Richard Clay Ltd, Bungay, Suffolk

for Louise Bennett and Edna Manley

Contents

Preface

After a while it seemed that many of the new Jamaican poems we had seen and liked were by women. Pam suggested the anthology and, disclaiming chauvinist intentions, asked Mervyn to share in the project. These are some poems we like. Each author is a woman who has not yet had a separate volume of her poems published.

Because these poets are all women, one may be tempted to raise the issue of whether they are 'poets who happen to be women', or something called 'woman poet'. But that is not the point. The poems are various. It is true that some of them express or explore vulnerability; some celebrate a strength that has made survival possible; some shrewdly attack the agents of their pain. But, as Jean D'Costa says, 'Terrible is the window in the mind': there is nothing limp in the responses of the poets here, nor is there any aggressive feminism in their work. They often demonstrate a striking 'distance' from their content: a kind of respectful concern that focuses more on the situation of the other than on the poet's *angst*. Olive Senior' 'Madman at Traffic Lights', Heather Royes' 'Theophilus Jones', Christine Craig's 'An Even Shape' and Lorna Goodison's

'Road of Dread' are cases in point. In their examination of inner and outer worlds, in their anatomizing of deceit, indifference, social injustice, their contemplation of time and death, these poets cannot be said to share a programme or a limited/limiting set of attitudes.

What these poets most noticeably share is a language, flexible in its range; they revel in the long continuum of Jamaican English; they push 'nation language' in all kinds of directions. 'I beat her down to a dollar fifty as she says I am clearly roots/I tell her curry goat irie', 'the music maker/steps into the dazzle of his sound', 'I crook a digit/Cool cool', 'Breed me/Life', 'Woman desist/he cannot hear your flesh', 'ef a ketch im/a mash im/ef a ketch im/a mash im', 'One day I trod wid I spar/Dung to Forbidden Territory', 'lord, old superstitions/are such lies'.

This anthology, we feel, is accessible to anybody in the community of readers. We hope that many of these poems give you pleasure in your contact with things that matter to the poets. That is the purpose. That is the point.

P.M.
M.M.

1

Jennifer Brown

Africa and the Caribbean

I came to you
fresh
dew wet
child of these islands
jewel of the Caribbean Sea
and you loved
my skin
like black sand beaches;
my hair
like coconut fibres
my lips
large and generous
tasting of sun and fruit.
You took me home
and together we dug
until we found
my long lost navel string;
we recalled the ceremonies
that had subsided in my skin;
I sang for you
my new songs
and we slept together at dawn.

It's Raining

it's raining
i'm sitting
thinking
of you
hoping that
that silver beads
washing my face
promise longer days
when afternoons' heat
swelters sweet
my skin
absorbing your heat

No Man's Land

Sorrow chloro-forms
my brain,

                and pain
like bright, hot car-lights
dull my eyes

            beet root
            starapple
            blood-flesh
the richest juice
of ripe fruit lies here
wasted . . .
not yet tasted . . .

Caviar and Sky Juice or C & S

Lances of light strike
the polished chrome of the Rolls Royce
that glided unseen through customs.
Power steered downhill
with effortless ease
by a manicured pinky
it glides past the bundle of filthy rags
who is compiling a treasury of waste
paper.

It lik a pot 'ole
one 'polish tin' wheel fly
offa de hand' cart
dat did mek outa
ole boawd
'trow-wey' tin
and Foreshore Road rubba
de sky-juice dat sell
nasty it up like
an 'im did tief de steerin' wheel.

The pinky curves the chrome round
a corner han' and bady strain to tun
de steerin' wheel chrome and cart
lik up!
sky juice fly in de face of chrome
car door opens, polished shoe tests
the ground
dutty barefoot step offa de rudda!
pure palava
FM plays "We shall overcome."

2

Christine Craig

Crow Poem

I want so much to put
my arms around you but
extended they are feathered
vanes, snapped, tatty things
no longer curving.

My voice wants to say things
about blue skies, blond sand,
yet a rasping, carrion croak
jets from my beak
sharp edged.

Condemned to live a life for which
I am ill suited, improperly
dressed. Perhaps there is out there
one crow, wheeling over the city dump
convinced she is a woman.

An Even Shape

Her garden looks in through my window
Criss-crossed by the white lattice.
Coolers they call them but they are also
Hiding places for small girls playing.

Her garden stands neatly round her house
Travels politely unto the verandah
To sit in pots or hang
Leafily down from large, earth coloured urns.

She lives with Mama, shepherding with her full body
The hesitant ins and outs of Mama's half-blind days.
Feeding her frail consciousness with edited Gleaner
    news
And homemade chicken soup.

In her home, borrowed children touched her china
    birds with hands
Wiped clean from eating sticky cakes, each with a
    cherry on top
Or press moist, breathless kisses round
The corners of her smile.

Sometimes she fills the spaces out
With music. Spreading out nostalgia through
Strings and flutes, old fashioned love songs
Of blue moons and forever and until.

Shameful peeping Tom, I sit silent in
My lattice watching the even shape of her days
To catch, just once, a wider open door behind
Her steady eyes.

But in her green edged privacy, self-contained
She keeps the half-drawn shutters of her life
Open just so, and mocks my greed and restlessness
With a calm refusal to be other than she seems.

New Year

The new year comes to meet us
wrapped in a gleaming cloak
of silver rain. All the obtuse,
divisive words of the old man
seem hollow now. Wet leaves,
white blossoms quiver a tremulous
clarity, a liquid mirror
of today's truth.

No tears for this aging lover,
our dry feet turn towards young hands.
Young, warm hands along our backs,
eyes brimming with green, white
and wet. In the still heart
of the mountain a stream grows
full with itself, hugging into
its curves slender grasses.

For just a little longer we straddle
the thin meridian. Roll on the tongue
an ashy taste of what has gone yet
part our lips for what is to come.

Hurry away old man with bitter eyes
the rain takes your footprints
before they are made. This year
you did not take the curve
from my child's body, for that
I give thanks. We will take growing
and singing into the quiet rain.

Poem

Stretching out across the windows of your face
I see a river washing down smooth, greying rocks.
I see a shameless, full-blown moon arrogantly
seeking out our naked feet
trumpeting the news of our humped knees.

I no longer care, keeping close my silence
has been a weight
a lever pressing out my mind.
I want it told and said and printed down
the dry gullies,
circled through the muddy pools
outside my door.
I want it sung out high by thin-voiced elders
front rowing murky churches
I want it known by grey faces queuing under greyer
        skies
in countries walking and sleeping with sleet and fog.
I want it known by hot faces pressed against
dust streaked windows of country busses.

And you must know this now.
I, me, I am a free black woman.
My grandmothers and their mothers
knew this and kept their silence
to compost up their strength,
kept it hidden
and played the game of deference
and agreement and pliant will.

It must be known now how that silent legacy
nourished and infused such a line
such a close linked chain
to hold us until we could speak
until we could speak out
loud enough to hear ourselves
loud enough to hear ourselves
and believe our own words.

Can you know this now that
I can choose this shaded place
under the seeing moon
only as that freedom shapes
our separate volition.

For D.S.

Once the stone god turned its
marble eyes and breathed out
moonlit fire on my thoughts.
Once I saw a river born, thrown
free from veins of chalky earth.
Once I even saw an egret
white throat streatched, swallow
the sunset all in one gulp.

But once, behind your sheltered eyes
I saw a flower curving from your palm.

For the Artists and Writers

So busy — late night pushing at the windows.
Spouses, indignant or resigned, register
a mute petition or slam another door.
In the days, jobs crowding out the sun,
forced activity round the sullen clock.
When we meet, warm enough smiles,
a calling card, we must meet
sometime. Sometime, as the grey curls
in your beard, as his body thickens
and little webs trickle from the corners
of my eyes. Sometime, as the young man
clothes his mind with un-shared songs.

We, writing black, the African experience,
flinging accusations at our colonial past,
vying with each other to vault most quickly
the sharp european fence. Rushing to see,
separately, whatever speaks of our warm,
black roots. Still the cold creeps up
through our careful behaviour.

It is at once more dangerous and more safe
to pour ourselves onto our flat lovers
who call us every night, urging to be covered,
to be owned by all the attention we reserve
lovingly for them. Are we such lonely cowards?

It used to be enough, but I no longer want
my portion meted out. I want now. A frightened
in the night child flinging wide the parent door.

An empty lover dry eyed at the window. A young mother howling in childbirth. A farmer thundering down the drought. Heavy, screaming want to push past the cool that we are.

Jean D'Costa

On Reading the Life of Mr. Silas Told:
Slave-trader, sailor, teacher & saint

How you call to me, call to me
Voices in sleep
Echoes of storms stilled, dusks, dawns ago
Before my own instant furled
Out of the turning world.

How you call to me, call to me
Voices long stilled
Under copper sun and brazen noon
Faces painted with fever's afternoon
Drugged with quinine, the Jesuit's bark.

How you call to me, call to me
Cries of the child
Left dying on road bank, river bank
In Volta, in Eire:
My feet cannot reach you through caverns of air.

How you call to me, call to me
Whispers of thoughts
Pressed to god, man and devil
Steel through the heart
Doll on a rope's end, excutioner's art.

How you call to me, call to me
Lightning of souls
Tossed sudden, chance begotten:
Your million days of men forgotten
Wielding axe, whip, or pen in the rage of the heart.

How you call to me, call to me
Dim echo of feet
On ways long since travelled
Through dread dreams long unravelled
For the loom no one sees.

Road

The road went through orange groves
Across bright fields--I can hear still
The laughter of the fieldhands,
Myself among them too
Busy talking around the baskets
Under the trees.
The road went round
Past Mr Eccleston's cottage
(He has had a stroke since)
And through a quarrel with a neighbour
Healed and sealed. Dogs bark
Through mist on the morning task,
The noonday meal; still on and on
With narrowing speed
Unrolls and falls
To this — a ribbon stretched to nothing.

In Memoriam

Terrible is the window in the mind:
Against the summer burnt hillside
Crows circle in the sleepy light.
Someone must carry on political dispute
For black and white.
My labour lies with the dappled land.
(Memory turns on such geometric hinges
We may open him both ways).
All the while crows circle
Sweeping broad swathes in July air.
Turn up stone and you will see a face
Close your eyes and you will hear
Voices in the blistered trees:
Particular incidents, clear as newsprint,
Glint from the edge of sight.
The half-heard noise,
The rustle of nameless feet.
The familiarity of strangers
Unlatch the window in the mind.

Consider an example:
This woman died young
And still her laughter echoes in the world.
Her grave is dusty and forgotten,
Her children grown and gone
Her household sold or given away;
All dispersed, disposed of without trace.
Yet, yet in the echoing place
All is lost — all is won.

For Hu, written at his house on June 9, 1977
> *Rose*

White rose, red rose
soul and ghost in the garden
Why, in that dim between day's going
I see a shape where a rose should be?
> *Green Rose*

Furled out of earthbrown
A sun's fantasy
Traced in molecules air-spun
Watched, hatched, insect-kissed
A promise, a green secret.
> *Flame Rose*

Terror came too sudden
Like morning spilled
Or lightning standing still
To laugh.
The still forest holds its breath
Throws fire in my face.
> *Yellow Rose*

Some say you will betray
Some say you will bring gold
But only blind men's hearts can tell
How the silk one walks
Currents of endless winds.
> *Last Rose*

Rose shape in the air where a rose should be,
Rosa munda,
Rosa Mundi —
Flower of Babylon and flower of Rome:
Open the door, open the door,
I will go home.

Lost, Never Found

"That is the place," said the Astronomer
Leaning from behind Arcturus
In earth's upper sky
"The planet where they lose things,
Where no one can find
Their lost knives, wives, dogs or hogs,
Their money or their lives
Once the desired object vanishes from sight.
I've studied them six million years
Since my promotion to this job.
Look —
All kinds of disappearances:
The crew of the *Marie Celeste*
Is only a splinter of the ships
Boats that went out on business or pleasure
Fishermen rich and poor
In canoes, kayaks, junks
Sailors of triremes
Sailors of submarines
(One lies in a valley
In the mountains of the sea)
Lost and never found.
And not only is the sea
Full of men who failed to answer letters
But consider the desert
Where on one occasion two valuable camels
Were wrongly assumed stolen,
The incident starting a tribal war
And never their bones seen
Or their lost footsteps found.

Children, too, have been one moment
All at play in the garden
And the next have stepped through
A door of air into the unknown.
Jewellery and keys have a way
Of departing for parts undisclosed
Without a message
Or a forwarding address.
Parcels go through the post
To the same destination
And somewhere there is wealth untold
Of all the money vanished
Out of wallets, banks, safes
From double-audited accounts
Of respectable merchant ventures
And other less respectable;
From the widow's purse
The collection plate
And every national treasury.
Computers have helped
To lose as much
As ever disappeared from the granaries
Of Thebes or Alexandria or Rome.
Then the names, the languages,
Even the very shapes of things
— The wheel was invented six times,
But who knows about the other five?
Brooches too have fallen in the grass
During processions and tea-parties
Cricket balls, golf balls, arrows and spears
Abound in the vanished place.

Manuscripts, vases, and the results of examinations
Sometimes a whole dinner service
With the Romanov crest
Or the mark of some potter
Working in a shed near Limoges.
Answers to sums
Have gone from exercise books overnight,
Along with Frisky,
Black and white dog with red collar
Please call Peter Brown.
As for the causes, the feuds,
The important issues of the day
Lost, never found
Under clouds of argument and gunsmoke
Untraceable forever
Even though thirty incidents in Budapest
And two in Vienna, six on an estate
Ten miles from Sarajevo
And eight conversations
Spoken in the Croat language
Have yet to be discovered
In the graveyards of the Somme.
So, too, is the week
Spent on a certain Caribbean island
Where the passionate embrace
Of two mutual strangers
Left behind a nameless son
To start a long tradition
Of unparented offspring.
For children mislay parents
Just as often as the other way around.

The worst is, to my mind,
The friendship that slips through the door
During an idle conversation
Runs down to the bus-station
Buys a one-way ticket
For some unknown location.
And their gods too, their gods
Also disappear from time and mind
Sometimes by force.
Yet every generation wonders
Where dreams come from,
Or those wholly unexpected moments on the road
When the heart flames with sudden gold.

4

Dorothea Edmondson

Petition

Be my centre,
My centrality

Be my anchor,
My anchorage

Through this instrument
Effect some purpose

Some meaning
Out of chaos.

Make me submit
Desire to your will

Knowing the world
Believing still.

Ground me to Truth
When I would rationalise

Ground me until I hide
My face from your eyes.

The Roots-man

On campus
they say he's
proceleusmatic.
Word word!
he likes it
and strikes the pose:
clothes like Nyerere,
guerilla cap,
pin-ups of Mao, Mau-Mau,
and a slogan —
watch, snoop, cool it,
when the time is ripe
we'll swipe.

In town
they say he's
charismatic:
Comrades, who is robbing you?
Who who who?
And you, black woman woman,
stand behind your man,
build your black man.

Black in his rebel roost
he's strangely subdued,
a red-haired woman rules the roost.
Her mistress-of-the-manor style
put to use
on servants, decor:
porcelain from Europe's salons

deck zebra skin tom-toms —
culture amalgamation —
she explains

He calls her his Union Jack
she calls him her black.
But when he's wracked
with rebel rage
she purrs, tiger in my cage,
when he nightly prays
to fix just that one imperialist,
when he struggles with that there flag,
she goads, fakir-nigger

Sheepskin

I loll on this rug
lumped like a slug
as cold as satisfied.

I roll round in woolly curls
plumb beneath the thick skin
(even the paws have turned limp)

Sweet Sin,
this sheepskin hid a sheep
a sheep in sheep's clothing.

Well I ate him,
O yes, I ate him up,
all of him in an evil hour,

His fabulous skin is mine
I stroke his form, trace
spine, hind, hind, spine.

Is there nothing more?

His heart was lust
his soul was mind,
mind mind the trap of our kind!

From the depths he'd cried Baaa.
That's all I can remember — Baaa.
Maybe that's all we were.

Safari

Bamboo roof
knarled contortions
a blue-green-luminous
sunless world
and gorillas.
Lord, have they been swinging through the centuries?

Leaves hiss
shadows quicken my pace forty four miles to flatland
there metal mirrors
game-shaped trees shade game
suntricks boggle eyes
peeled by pothole — vigilance
socket-dance
a flow of birds is a streaming rainbow.

Cows
the arch-horned came from Egypt
as the ancestors of these
herders light as reeds.
Tourists snapshot their
nonchalance
would patent the 'technique'
given a chance

Hills
hills hills with wispy haloes
all sleepy old volcanoes . . .
Lord, how old is Africa?
Four a.m. and Mt. Bufumbira's erupting stars
morning drips diamonds
bless the Lord
bless his Holy Name

the old man said it's always the same
new every morning and nothing new

The old man?
I met him in Kisoro
he was near ninety
unproteined.
This old man threw spears.
They quivered on mark yards away

For me?
Did I like did I like?
The old man was a ladysman though bent like
middle-C

He played the enanga stomping
stamping
moaning crooning gurgling through stumpy gum

Did I like?
Did I like?
I liked I liked I
Danced and danced
Dervishly wild suntranced
Till Sorghum Millett & Maize
Danced "round 'an 'round 'an blurred . . .

For Dad

A slab marks the spot.
It's chipped. Climate
or the careless chop
of a machete . . .
wonder what next,
when this tomb crumbles what object
what sign to define his plot?
A headstone? A simple one
above those weeds? People tether
cattle to headstones, they
soon crack, crumble, decay
like everything else . . .

I'll let the weeds spread over
his grave. Nature blooms its own cover
he was a nature-lover.

Yet the woof and warp
of his sixty-five years are epitaphed
in few words — Dad is dead.

This is his tomb, marble
unyielding as love petrified.
All memories died
when he did. I try to recall home.
Nothing flickers, all's ashes to ashes,
the faded album did better — it burned.

Pretense flown, I look around:
all's decay all's rundown
Let go Dorothea let go
There's nothing here. In this loam
his flesh dissolved — weeds
are flowering from it to fatten
cattle. Futile, just futile
your limp bouquet to pay
respects (respects!), is.
All's decay all's rundown.

Get out, move on, look ahead
let the past shroud its dead.

Walked out the macca-ridden
cattle-ridden, dungful graveyard
knowing I have returned at last
but cannot go back; the past
is there behind that reclaimed track,
it's there, a four-eyed, square, phantom,
far-away, crowding-in,
forgiven yet unforgiving.

Black Art

Hair-springs
springs
round my fingers
magnets down
the long strong neck
beneath this chest
Africa's heart beats
black love
black magic
black art
in this dimple
simply snipped
chiselled loving-
ly I play
link-me.
Pagan god Bone
stokes thighs honed
boned to murderous
strength
something's flickering
tongues of fire
eyes slit secrets speak
love hate create
I quail through nights
God is a Terrible Fear
the rites the rites
dreaded and dear

5

Lorna Goodison

Gordon Town Morning

Gordon Town this morning
Was the dalliance of Ralph Campbell
in slack flirtation with a fat cloud.
She's lifted her dress
and is wheeling her cumulous frocktail
over the heads of the church and courthouse
spires.

The wheels direct themselves
over the wedge of that same bridge
where Nigel my brother
And I was his fat dreaming sister
would wait for our morning drive.
"Morning Children" . . . "Morning sir"
                . . . "Morning sir"
The silence changing gears, till
Goodbye Children . . . Goodbye sir
              . . . Goodbye sir.

The first poetry then of gold filigree poui
I longed to live at Mill-in-Spring
a displaced heroine with a faceless lover.

Years later throughout the same streets a frightened
      bride.
Now a woman with a face that has earned every line.
It was nothing my springtime, it was nothing my smile
She loved a young warrior. Her brother took a bride.
It was nothing my brother/companero it happened
      before
And Wai Rua does not lead to home anymore.

For A.N. and the Others

This day, me rural
revolutionary
go deal with a peasant
Bout a feeder road.
Now me sleep mongst Jew
Kibbutz my pride a Israel
"to the fields"
my head agrarian
I know
Textbook, how it grow.

Like a sudden test
the sky wrinch!
and lash forward a rain
just so
I mek fi shelter
when the countryman
say
"is ongle rain me son,
it clean yu know."

It beat like wire
and connect with mi mole
but the bush man know

Him chop a banana leaf
and hand me a living
green shield
against the sky's attack

"Yes a road through ya
would a good yu know
now is the weather
when carrot can grow".

Ocho Rios

A conquistador hit by the muse who gives names
tongue-tied eight rivers together.

The British, recognizing that the Spaniards
had the all-time hit "Arawak Genocide",
let that name be. But wrought some name calling
of their own.

"so how black, black man like you and me
name Goodison and Montgomery?"

In Ocho Rios market I ask the cookshop lady

"how much for the curry goat?"
"Three dolla"
"Fi wan curry goat"
"A four dolla fi tourist sista".

I beat her down to a dollar fifty.
she says I am clearly roots.
I tell her the curry goat irie.

Its true. Its taste strokes my senses gone wild from
            smells
astringent vegetables and heaps of earthwrapped yams.

The crotchety old maid selling lace and the one from
            St. Mary,
Face oiled with Necromancy, selling asophetida and
            mustard yellow
sulphur and Kananga Water and frankincense and
            myrrh.

The sign in the square says "Tourism, not socialism"
and though I eat this curry sitting on a feed bag from
            Florida

This market belies your investments Isabella
And you Combulous, whose aims conjuncted with
            Venn and Penables,
which Colonizer is winning in Ocho Rios?

For R & R in the Rain

Knock, knock . . . who's there?
R & R in the rain (add failed)
But that would be jumping the gun.
But then I never saw the gun
till he clicked it.
I never felt the gun till
my temples were nearly overturned
by this money snatcher.
All week the house hugged me
The walls stood straight duty
for me
The windows grateful for my openness.
All week just me and the cow lowing
and the tyger striped anteater
and the solitaire.
Just me and my bush family.
The rain mixed your knock
with equal parts credibility
and damp obscurity.

The knock knock joke was on me
I opened to your face set
in brute calm
"Ah cum fi yu and the munny".

I fought you.

For breaking the friendship with the house and me
For what might have been the painless delivery
of a poem.

For the week's harassment from the mad rass woman
For the dishonest men who ripped me off in loudness
        name
For victimization and unprincipled dealings.
For the system that breeds lost lumpen men like you.
For my mother who work all her life to rest,
and can't rest yet.
For my brother who fought a war for strangers and
        lost
For all the times I smiled when I should have spat!

I BEAT YOU!

For My Mother (May I Inherit Half Her Strength)

my mother loved my father
I write this as an absolute
in this my thirtieth year
the year to discard absolutes

he appeared, her fate disguised,
as a sunday player in a cricket match,
he had ridden from a country
one hundred miles south of hers.

She tells me he dressed the part,
visiting dandy, maroon blazer
cream serge pants, seam like razor,
and the beret and the two-tone shoes.

My father stopped to speak to her sister,
till he looked and saw her by the oleander,
sure in the kingdom of my blue-eyed grandmother.
He never played the cricket match that day.

He wooed her with words and he won her.
He had nothing but words to woo her,
On a visit to distant Kingston he wrote,

'I stood on the corner of King Street and looked,
and not one woman in that town was lovely as you".

My mother was a child of the petite bourgeoisie
studying to be a teacher, she oiled her hands
to hold pens.
My father barely knew his father, his mother died
            young,
he was a boy who grew with his granny.

My mother's trousseau came by steamer through the
            snows of Montreal
where her sister Albertha of the cheekbones and the
perennial Rose, combed Jewlit backstreets with French-
turned names for Doris' wedding things.

Such a wedding Harvey River, Hanover, had never seen
Who anywhere had seen a veil fifteen chantilly yards
            long?
and a crepe de chine dress with inlets of silk godettes
and a neck-line clasped with jewelled pins!

And on her wedding day she wept. For it was a brazen
            bride in those days
who smiled.

and her bouquet looked for the world like a sheaf of
          wheat
against the unknown of her belly,
a sheaf of wheat backed by maidenhair fern, represent-
          ing Harvey River
her face washed by something other than river water.

My father made one assertive move, he took the
          imported cherub down
from the height of the cake and dropped it in the soft
          territory
between her breasts . . . and she cried.

When I came to know my mother many years later,
          I knew her as the figure
who sat at the first thing I learned to read: "SINGER",
          and she breast-fed
my brother while she sewed; and she taught us to read
          while she sewed and
she sat in judgement over all our disputes as she sewed.

She could work miracles, she would make a garment
          from a square of cloth
in a span that defied time. Or feed twenty people on a
          stew made from
fallen-from-the-head cabbage leaves and a carrot and a
          cho-cho and a palmful
of meat.

And she rose early and sent us clean into the world
          and she went to bed in
the dark, for my father came in always last.

There is a place somewhere where my mother never
      took the younger ones
a country where my father with the always smile
my father whom all women loved, who had the
      perpetual quality of wonder
given only to a child . . . hurt his bride.

Even at his death there was this "Friend" who stood
      by her side,
but my mother is adamant that that has no place in
      the memory of
my father.

When he died, she sewed dark dresses for the women
      among us
and she summoned that walk, straight-backed, that she
      gave to us
and buried him dry-eyed.

Just that morning, weeks after
she stood delivering bananas from their skin
singing in that flat hill country voice

she fell down a note to the realization that she did
not have to be brave, just this once
and she cried.

For her hands grown coarse with raising nine children
for her body for twenty years permanently fat
for the time she pawned her machine for my sister's
Senior Cambridge fees
and for the pain she bore with the eyes of a queen

and she cried also because she loved him.

The Road of Dread

That dey road no pave
like any other black-face road
it no have no definite colour
and it fence two side
with live barbwire.

And no look fi no milepost
fi measure you walking
and no tek no stone as
dead or familiar

for sometime you pass a ting
you know as . . . call it stone again
and is a snake ready fi squeeze yu
kill yu
or is a dead man tek him
possessions tease yu
Then the place dem yu feel
is resting place because time
before that yu welcome like rain,
go dey again?
bad dawg, bad face tun fi drive yu underground
wey yu no have no light fi walk
and yu find sey that many yu meet who sey
them understand
is only from dem mout dem talk.
One good ting though, that same treatment
mek yu walk untold distance
for to continue yu have fe walk far
away from the wicked.

Pan dis same road ya sista
sometime yu drink yu salt sweat fi water
for yu sure sey at least dat no pisen,
and bread? yu picture it and chew it accordingly
and some time yu surprise fi know how dat full
man belly.

Some day no have no definite colour
no beginning and no ending, it just name day
or night as how you feel fi call it.

Den why I tread it brother?
well mek I tell yu bout the day dem
when the father send some little bird
that swallow flute fi trill me
And when him instruct the sun fi smile pan me first.

and the sky calm like sea when it sleep
and a breeze like a laugh follow mi.
or the man find a stream that pure like baby mind
and the water ease down yu throat
and quiet yu inside.

and better still when yu meet another traveller
who have flour and yu have water and man and man
make bread together.
And dem time dey the road run straight and sure
like a young horse that can't tire
and yu catch a glimpse of the end
through the water in yu eye
I won't tell yu what I spy
but is fi dat alone I tread the road.

6

Sally Henzell

That Summer

that summer
or the long hot drought
I used to watch you
watering the grass
and flowers whose names you
did not know
that was the summer
we were poor
and you built a daydream
out of nothing
that became our life
waiting for the rain

Where I Live

enchanted
is a place
where I live
in a space
pricked
by stars that are suns

to needle the night
shrill as crickets
inching in
under trees
that reach out
lace fingers
to touch
other poets
such as snails
in the grass

Duppy Umbrella*

Duppy Umbrella, Frail Messenger
from the Mother
in the magical morning
you are born of
dew-drops and dank places
mushrooming
out of the earth
a small cloud
a bomb sent from Jah
to shatter the mind like an accident
and replace it with another puzzle

*Local Name for hallucinogenic mushroom.

Stones

although it seems
the world has come between us
stones
and a mere mention of miles
cannot
stop the breath
the way
I've known it
suspended
between your monumental eyes

Blue

Blue was wild
and Blue was free
he used to walk the woods
speaking his version
a dub of blue
one day they locked him up
he nearly suffocated
behind the bars and concrete
now he's out
he sleeps gratefully
under cardboard
beneath the stars

On Tour: Boston '74

lured
out on to the black stage
by the animal cry
of a people
lusting to see their own soul's
mirror
the music maker
steps into the dazzle of his sound
spilling spells
flooding worlds
building highs
with the magic reflection of dreamers

7

Bridget Jones

Naming the Work

He wrote his titles on neat white cards
Cut and shuffled the pile
Made a fan Chose a card
Struck out the vowels
Burnt the upper case.

After eighteen months
The publisher
Between one whisky and the next
Decreed:
Page one line one. Use that.

Study fe Teacher

Some thicken palms with cutlass and hoe
Split fingers with suds
Slash nails with fish-knife
Stun with stones.

My trade gives the mind no ease
Stuns the heart
And slowly clogs the lungs:
Black board white dust.

Chores and Worse

In the silent house
I hear the cat's tongue on fur

The window pane is clean
Dry herbs taste again of green

With a faint sigh
The tomato loses its scalp

Now the steel is bright
I am quartering my baby's neck and back
Not a splinter.

For Madame Camille M.

His study silvers over now with dust
You pour the syrup to meet their rum
But that hat once daring into sepia fades
Fierce pilgrims come to scoff at the fine script
Ground out between the mill-stones
Where time tethered his eyes.

The words slip between your knotted fingers
And stumble down the stair
While the plant in the window puts out a frailer second
          bloom

Thermo-static

Last night was
Hot hot
Braided your body hair
Right down
Sucked your left toe
Right off
My sweet lies
Your matt eyes
Our wet sweat gleaming

Then sleep
thick
as red pea soup
knotted with dumpling

Today
We pass
By Barclays Bank
Your left lid flickers
I crook a digit
Cool cool.

Knucklebone Soup

Under thatched shelters in a dozen islands
Chack-chack maracas chatter and hiss.

Crack the Haitian gourd --
No seeds are there
Only the limestone pebbles
from a cemetery plot.

To a Tune by Jimmy Cliff

So many rivers
When the bamboo sinks
Give me your hand

So many rivers
When the boat is lost
Breathe in the light

So many rivers
When the black rain blows
Shelter me.

The brown water
Returns no dead.

8

Sandy McIntosh

Lost, One Soul

I lost my soul in a fit of temper
I threw it at somebody's head
and slammed out
without a second thought

Then I dumped it in a wastebin
along with a love I said I was finished with

I sandpapered my spirit
with a million
bitter barbs
and sent it into orbit
and substituted
guilt instead

My soul went cold
with memories of old friends and kin
who never expected
to be neglected,
and resolutions
I'd eluded

Then one day
I went to feed it
and it was gone

and now I hear it howling
in the wind outside
in the nights
in the hills

and I get the chills inside

and hide
in something that's not important
and it's four in the morning
before I can get warm enough
to weep enough
to fall asleep

Darn!

night people
we're not bright
in the morning
(yawning)
if you're wise to us
you can tell us by the eyes
(bleary)
and our air of weary
snappiness
after a blissful
night
of being awake
when it makes us
happy to be . . .

seeing
the
calm darkness
outside our light
hearing the still
thinking deep
scorning sleep
being alone
or being together
writing poems
or whatever . . .
feeling good now
tasting delights
the dawn puts to flight

moon
lighting our way home
coolness
soothing our tangled nerves
stepped on all
daylong

what went wrong?
who gave control
to those ol'
day people?

No Way

Chasing my tail
failing
to shake
the fears
breaking
changing gears
too fast
masterminding
escape routes
and futilely
carrying myself along
to haunt
each new me
see-
ing
my pain
in other peoples'
eyes
that's where it lies
thought I was
OK
No way.

Siamese Comfort

The jasmines came to me
a little while ago.
Before that
my cat and I

surveyed the pink and orange
corner of the sky
while the little palm
turned black and silhouetted
and I thought about my life
and wished that I could die
and he shut his eyes
and told me not to cry.

Where?

I don't think anymore
I just wonder
out yonder
and back
inside me

I'm wide of the mark
I guess;
it never
adds up
to 'yes'
just yesterdays

. . . ways it could
have been
different
and why it went
the way it did . . .

Who hid
the meaning?

Cleaning out my mind
never gets me
anywhere
any more.

9

Alma Mock Yen

Thinking of Guillen's "My Last Name"

Write it
I am black
Living it
I go white at the womb
I am we
I cannot reach the theys
My bloods mix milk and sugar.
When I write —
And by their carefully planned way
I write the codes which shackle me forever
To that half-of-past which strode the peaks
Alone —
I right my self,
Break free,
Dive into the blue treasure that is Africa and me
And for a moment only
Wear
The honey-black diaspora in my hair
Fragile black foam crowns my beauty's ebonies
But
Back upon the beach.
On shore
The winds blow all the foam away

And I walk
Home
Wearing a million faces

Notice: All those who want to send Christmas
Greetings Please Sign Below:

It hangs there glitterlessly
While the year picks flaming blossoms for storage
In cupboards of seeds.

I hang
Lustreless,
Awaiting repeats of the same old-year problems
Which lit up, flickered,
Blew the fuse of my heart.

Very few greetings were sent.

Happy New Year

CCC Silos, 1975

Beside the sea they mixed the rivers' loam
With limestone from the mountain clinker-veined
Man hours the wounded quarry raped and tamed
To build a fat, industrial storage dome.

Time's fingers mixed the seasons with the salt
Clocks punched at legal tender's constant ring
The silos' bellies kept the precious thing
Cement for sale, exchange to fill the vault.

The passing seasons mellowed the sea's salt.
Then one still evening moonlight sucked away the
      sand
The engineers are puzzled to this day

The silos leaning on an open fault
Cost millions more to blast, reduce to dust
Back to the mountains blowing an ancient smile at us.

Lines in the Night

I am wallowing
in my store
unsure
that tomorrow
can afford me
I am sinking
in my bed
back to the fountainhead.
Breed me
Life
I am dead
unsaid
the letters
overlying me

No one will find me

Late Show

while i was sleeping
women shifted
the pawns   kings left
queens   lost
the stables

minstrels washed
faces   black
paint dis-   appeared
in the midnight of S-bends
the sons of the midnight
roared   au
naturel

relevance
germinated
sprouting
who   why
when   why
why   why   why?
knitting points
of departure   dropping
stitches
while i
sleeping

while i was sleeping
excesses went into
labour   pain
wracked the cliches

words spun
b u r s t
contracted
a   borted
verses changed   me
tre
students burnt robes
to my snoring
the pronoun hic
cupped   i and i
and i
fast   asleep
when   trans
mission
ended

Lament for a Half-Done Dream

so light
it lies here
like death
gathering
stars
gathering
venom
a sleep
without
wings

wending its way
deep
inside
wounding
the vacuum
of my peace
never ending
not quite beginning
a snake
never striking
a wake
for someone
asleep

the child cries, "Mummy I want water"
the night breaks like a
bubble, deep down
the rib cage cracks
like eggshell ·
oozes
a dream
lost in space
no meaning

10

Velma Pollard

Moonhope

Casuarinas brush
the edge of moon
and click their lenses
now before the deep
blue tinged with orange
nightmare shroud
cloud masks her

But soon
the moon her light
confounds the blue
scatters the orange
blazes forth
untinged by blue
untinged by orange now

Now casuarinas
gaze their wonder
climbing at the moon
her graceful distancing
and casuarinas wait
to catch
that shining edge . . . tomorrow

Bud/Unbudded

This bud beheld me watch
her glory folded
This bud beheld me move one minute spot in time
Unbudded/Outrose/her petals myriading . . .

This flower sees me watch
her glory flaunted
This flower hears me pause and knows I pause
to grieve for her tomorrows spaces.

Martha

Woman desist
he cannot hear your flesh
your tongue and well-springs
over-elocute
her spirit speaks.

He tunes you out
but swings you in
with habit thrust
another she infuses all his sense
whose spirit throbs
and blows his body
in your mind
woman desist
and live.

After Cages

Behind remembered Sunday papers
sits my father's grunts.
rain patter or the sharp uneven crunch
of children's feet toeing the gravel
Mulvina's off again (I hear her say) . . .
Did you remember, called your mother yesterday? . . .
and chews more firmly on his latest pipe.

After the patter
after children's tired toes
the silent Sunday
thunders this bird's exit
leaving her window-peering silent
newly old.

Someday I'd say
she'll up and go
leaving him window-peering under rain
drops chewing pipes
at home
no going when its no one that you are leaving.

Behind these Sunday papers
sits my father's silence now
hearkening the raindrops' patter
or the pebbles empty of remembered feet;
parsley and mint fragrant where I remember
brown pipes and brown tobacco littering the ash

Soundless we sit
silent and impotent
who is Mulvina?
where his mother now?
I know no questions
feel no urge to learn
too late I know
he needs to answer
lonely women newly old
but oddly silenced now
stretched out beside the flowers
boxed brown in aged mahogany.

for "Time" Oct 18, 1976

Tonight my love
the drums are cold
and drum-sticks sickly
lean about the corner
where my father
warmed his ageing skin
or fed his eyesight
on the city sprawling
underneath our hill

the drums are cold;
went cold beneath my hands
the moment that his spirit fled;

spoke nothing mindless of our care
and mindless of the white libations
sprinkled from my lips . . .

the drums will speak again
tomorrow when his body underearths;
the drums must speed him
home outside that other hill
that looks over our valley
and the sea

and afterwards
these drums will only speak
beyond tomorrow
when his children
live my father's dreams
beyond the time
when fires flaming on his land
blacken what must burn out
to burst another better
living for my father's seed

then drums my love
will sweeten all this hill
and hark my father's spirit
home from fruitless wanderings
to sit beside its pulse
and hear my children sing
and watch their fingers
speak these very drums he loved
then joy my father's shade.

Fly

ef a ketch im
a mash im
ef a ketch im
a mash im
ef a ketch im . . . .

Will you walk into my parlour
Said the spider to the fly
It's the prettiest snugliest parlour
That ever you did spy . . .
And I
the fly
inspecting your web
this skein now then that
put my
microscope eye
through its intricate weave
saw valleys of cloud
blue and serene
saw acres of grass
sheltered and green.
Ephemeral and light
I rested my life
and dazzled
I watched
you wove me inside
and dazzled
I slept
my crysalis sleep . . . . .
                * * *

I woke up inside
no more dazzled and green.
Awake and alert
unfolding my wings
I stretched . . . . . .
But your skeins
not delicate now
resistant and strong
they wove me inside
I am trapped
I can't move
I can't butterfly
fly . . . .

And you
perched outside
your eyes large and clear
you see acres of green
you see valleys of cloud
you can move
you can fly . . . .
Now I look
through the web
I look into the void
I see numberless flies
training microscope eyes
through intricate weave
ANANSI I cry
ANANSI — SI — SI I hear
the sky is too vast
how it scatters my cry

the sky is too clear
it hides my despair
they can't hear
they can't see
with their microscope eye . . . .

ef a ketch im
a mash im
ef a ketch im
a mash im

A ketch im . . . im . . . im

11

Heather Royes

Death Came to See Me in Hot Pink Pants

Last night, I dreamt
that Death came to see me
in hot-pink pants
and matching waistcoat too.
He was a beautiful black saga boy.
Forcing open the small door of my wooden cage,
he filled my frame of vision
with a broad white smile,
and as he reached for my throat,
the pink sequins of his shoulders
winked at me.

Last night, I dreamt
that Death came to see me in hot-pink pants.
He was a beautiful black saga boy.
And I hit him with a polished staff
of yellow wood,
and he went down.
But as he reached for me once more,
Laughing, laughing that saga boy laugh,
I awoke, holding myself,
unable to breathe.
How beautiful was Death
in hot-pink pants with matching waistcoat too.

Hotel in Havana

At four in the morning,
the busboys danced a flamenco
on the patio in the dark.
Looking down from the window,
I could not see them through
the thick, night-blackened palms,
but the rythmn of their heels and hands
staccato-ed up to me.

Sun-strobes began to light Havana Harbour,
throwing up rays behind Morro Castle,
sending stripes streaking
across the flat water,
and brightening the wide
empty boulevards.

The hotel sat, with peeling facades,
like an aging prostitute
reflecting days of decadence
before the Revolution.
Decadence haunted the high ceilings,
swung from the chandeliers
and sent ghostly laughter
whirling down the long corridors.

I love you, Havana,
with your ice cream parlour lines
in 1950's fashions.
I love your bony, bare streets,

cleansed of urban crowds
rushing nowhere to do nothing.
Your once elegant mansions
now festooned with lines of washing,
your children with tomorrow faces,
your people and your austere dignity.

Sweet black coffee and harsh cigarettes
beside the pool where once
fat, white tourists bathed.
Workers on holiday vouchers
with un-hotel like faces
wandering through the lobby.
The girl with the red Defenso Militar
armband who wore dangling earrings,
stockings, high-heeled shoes,
and chatted with her friend
behind the cigarette counter.

Later, in the evening,
two sharks swam lazily in the harbour,
while downstairs in the cabaret,
the rhumba dancer,
left over from other days,
shook out his equally ancient
black costume and prepared
his strands of hair.
There will be cassava and rice
on the menu again tonight.

When Folks Like You Have Birthdays

When folks like you have birthdays,
the country should fire a 21-gun salute,
shout hip-hip-hurrah,
and blow all the ships' whistles in Kingston Harbour.

Instead, we had a curfew — a sign of changing times.
Yet, it was most appropriate
that on your birthday we should feel
the changing times,
the crackle and crumble
of the old, hard crust
as the new breaks through.

So, on your birthday,
which was a nice enough May morning wrapped in
        blue,
we were unable to bring on the 21-gun salute
(though guns were firing),
shout hip-hip-hurrah (though shouting was heard),
or blow all the ships' whistles (though whistles were
        blown).

But as the curfew ended,
and the tanks crunched their way home,
the soldiers and policemen wearily shouldered their
        rifles,
and Kingston was back to normal . . . . .
we thought of you.

Theophilus Jones Walks Naked Down King Street

On Monday, October 18th,
Theophilus Jones took off
his asphalt-black, rag-tag pants
and walked naked down King Street.
It was a holiday —
and only a few people saw
his triumphant march,
his muscular, bearded-brown body,
his genitals flapping in front.
Theophilus Jones had wanted
to do this for a long time.

At Tower and King, three carwash boys
shouting "Madman!", followed him to Harbour Street,
but seeing his indifference, turned
and dribbled back up the road.
Down on the Ferry Pier, a handful of people
waiting for the boat, stared out to sea
but did not see
Theophilus enter the water.
He walked out as far as possible,
then began to swim, strongly and calmly,
into the middle of the harbour.
Eventually, way out in the deep,
he stopped,
floated for a while, enjoying the sun,
watched a plane take off from the green-rimmed palisades,
and then, letting himself go,
allowed the water
to swallow him up.

Theophilus Jones went down
slowly,
slowly his bent legs, slowly
his arms above his head,
slowly his locksed hair,
slowly.
Until nothing could be seen of him.
Some orange peel, an old tin-can
and a sea-saturated cigarette box
floated over his demise,
while nearby,
a kingfisher — scavenging for sprats
on a low current — veered down
and landed,
in a spray of sunlit water.

12

Olive Senior

Epitaph

Last year the child died
we didn't mourn long
and cedar's plentiful

but that was the one
whose navel-string we buried
beneath the tree of life

lord, old superstitions
are such lies.

Searching for Grandfather

I
In Colón I searched for my
grandfather without connection.
Not even the message of his
name in the phone book.

II
Along the Line I found my
grandfather disconnected
at Culebra.

Hacking at the Cut
he coughed his brains loose
and shook

(but it was only malaria).

You're lucky they said as they
shipped him home on the deck
of the steamer, his mind
fractured but his fortune intact:
Twenty-eight dollars and two
cents. Silver.

III
What he had learnt to do really
well in Colón was wash corpses.
At home the village was too poor
to patronise. He was the one
that died.

His sisters laid him out in a
freshly-made coffin and cried:
there was nothing left of the
Silver Roll to weigh down his
eyes

for although his life has been
lacking in baggage, they didn't
want him to see that on this
voyage out he still travelled
steerage.

Ancestral Poem

I
My ancestors are nearer
than albums of pictures
I tread on heels thrust
into broken-down slippers

II
My mother's womb impulsed
harvests perpetually. She
deeply breathed country air
when she laboured me.

III
The pattern woven by my
father's hands lulled me
to sleep. Certain actions
moved me so: my father
planting.

When my father planted
his thoughts took flight.
He did not need to think.
The ritual was ingrained
in the blood, embedded
in the centuries of dirt
beneath his fingernails
encased in the memories
of his race.

(Yet the whiplash of my
father's wrath rever-
berated days in my
mind with the inten-
sity of tuning forks.
He did not think.
My mother stunned wept
and prayed Father
Forgive Them knowing not
what she prayed for).

One day I did not pray.
A gloss of sunlight through
the leaves betrayed me so
abstracted me from rituals.
And discarded prayers and
disproven myths
confirmed me freedom.

IV
Now against the rhythms
of subway trains my
heartbeats still drum
worksongs. Some wheels
sing freedom, the others:
home.

Still, if I could balance
water on my head I can
juggle worlds
on my shoulders.

Prayer

Pecharies
tackling the
hawks crying
in gunsights
casting
shadows

keep these
from our door
spare us skyfall
except rain

Lord, let no
danger lurk
in trumpet trees
and Rolling Calves
be not true

children save
from early dying
casting shadows

send a sign

let your glory
shine through clouds
beyond pecharies

And What of the Headlines?

In a perfect
equilibrium
like snow
and silence
I await
your gentle
coming
    — Calling
      of voices
      across
      silence —
Beyond the vapors
of your breath
other voices
calling
      calling
across
delinquent fences
from the gutters
of the all-night
streets
    — My anxieties
      are
      fanned
      alive.
Last night a girl screamed.
Thirty-eight shutters
flew shut. Everyone

watched television
until it was
all over.
This morning they
wash blood from the streets
making virgin paths
for early risers
   — The knife
     rose
     and fell
     rose
     and fell
     like the rhythm
     of your
     breathing
Now in the quiet dawn
you ask me:
Why are you anxious
Why are you sad
Why mustn't we talk
of Love?

Madman at Traffic Lights

When the Eye
turns red
you know
snake
shudders

and goes
still again
so you
stride
out and
in and
out its
coils to
charm it
to do
tricks
for you
But fearing
dread-
ness in
that one
red eye
the snake
goes
thrashing
to sal-
vation
as the eye
winks
green
again
You
on the edge
of in
and out

you
barely
miss
the hiss
of death
again
Triumphant
you shake
rattles

Albert Street

Rain ceases
with the coming
of the children

all the tired streets now
are filled with children's cries

they skitter like leaves
down the afternoon streets
all the innocent streets
of the world

Alas

all this early promise
of sunlight remains
largely unfulfilled

in undeclared wars
this May-be generation
these Now-smiling children

will fall, like raindrops.

13

Colleen Smith-Brown

Invitation

Will you come too?
It isn't far
Just a few steps
Down the road
Where green ferns cling
To a broken, crumbling wall
And the dismal, deserted nest
Tilts crazily
In the naked, withered branches.

Heart Grieves

Heart grieves
Echoing softly through the songs
Of wrongs long hushed up.
Like petals through the air
Sifting
Drifting into an eternity
Fall softly
To die
Heart grieves.

Burden

Harnessed between
The shafts of day and night
I pull the burden of Life
Unwillingly.

Tree

I am a tree —
Not the tender seedling
Young, vulnerable.

Nor the supple sapling
Flirting, flaunting
Greenery in the wind.
I am a tree —
I am a tree —
Broken, gnarled
Rooted fingers
Clutching desperately to my soil.
Battered, bruised shoots
Struggling fiercely towards the sun.

I am the tree
You chopped.

14

Cyrene Tomlinson

Foam, Foment, Ferment

White-white deh a mi mout cawna,
For a so-so shartrige and starvation awn ya.
Ten day now mi a have diarrhea,
An nat even likkle raw flour fi ease de pressha.
Mi tripe dem twis up
Mi belly a roll
A so-so gas fullup mi guthole.
Man can dribe dem car pan gas
But mi nuh car, so mi cyan wuk pan dat.

Miss Cassie use fi mek Johnny cake
An ketch it up with roas salfish
Now all she have is pure bellyache
Far nutten nuh inna har showcase.

An all di official dem a do
Is siddung wid "a nuh mi, a yu"
So dem call fi di whole heapa ism
All mi can see is pure "pass-di-buck-ism"
Big man dis an big man dat
All mi a hear a so-so chat
Dis one did do an dat one did sey
Wile fi mi pat empty, nutten in deh
Mi clothes dem dutty, cyan go nuhwey.

Joe-Joe naw wuk, dat mek it wuss
Nuh money nuh deh, de whole a wi bruk
Meanwhile dat dem belly pack
Yu nuh believe, check roun a back
Wey dem put out fi garbage or gi dem pet
All one whole a week mi nuh see dat yet.

How long wi fi put up wid dis candishan?
Wi is animal, candemn to starvashan?
Marley sey man hungry, man bex!
An dat nuh lie, a gaspel tex!
But ef wi nuh get something fi boost wi spirit
Nuh Jamaica nah lef fi wi pickney inherit
Far as a swear pan Bogle, Garvey and Busta grave
Wi look like wi headin right back to de cave
An wen dat happen, den a deh it a go deh
Wile beas' inna jungle woan bexxa dan wi. Aoh!

Dis Hypocrisy

Shock an outrage
Is wey dem sey dem feel
Wen de Big Man bite dus
Unda de gunman heel

Hear dem as dem call fi vengeance
Becaw a smaddy af importance

Candemnashan
Damnashan
Indignashan
Fretrashan
Dem sey dis t'reaten de 'ole Nashan

Mi 'ear de news
De official decree
De Man must get
Official ceremony

Shock an outrage mi . . . !
Official funaral? Nat a blas' ! ! !

What is dis hypocrisy? !

De fambily know betta
Far mi was dis gwine write a letta
Wen mi tek up de paypa an see de story
Sey de fambily a buried im privitely

But what a pieca hypocrisy ! !

An wen gunman a out-out poor people like flea
De official dem sey nieda dow nar dee
Wi dis lef fram de morgue to de cemetry
Dem good fi doan' even hear bout we

De workas stap wuk sey a bex dem bex
An dem a wanda who shall be de nex
But wen poor people baddy fulla bullet 'ole
Who strike fi we? Nat a dyam soul
Bassman doan even know wi pan payroll

What is dis hypocrisy? !

Mi nuh have nutten gains' Ogilvie
An mi naw talk true malice yu si,
Far wat dem do to de poor man
It grieve mi too, you undastan?

But mi cyan stan dis hypocrisy ! !

Far de way dem gwan ova dis man
A nuh so dem gwan ova ghetto man

Ef dem dida shock an outrage fi alla we
Den de nashan wudda have betta security
Far de official dem know wat cause dis calamity

Now de gunman dem dis a laugh
Fi see de style dem a pull awf

What is dis hypocris*y*? ! !

Bway, dankey seh dis worl nuh level
Special to who carry pickaxe an shovel
Fi wi name spell Nonentity
Fi wi name nuh spell Ogilvie

What is dis hypocrisy? ! !

An dem a call fi unity? ! !

Down wid dis hypocrisy! ! ! ! ! !

Message from the Grave

Watchya nuh–
I live inna de ghetto.
Is deh I bawn.
Is deh I find a dawta wey nuh shame fi talk to I
Before I wash I face and comb I hair.
Is deh I siddung pan de gate an tek een de scene.

Is deh I grow. Inna de ghetto.
Come hear bullet zing crass I ears,

Dig up hole inna de board house wey I
An I old lady an I sista an bredda dem call home.
Nex mawnin ded baddy roun de back.
Come see man kick dung de door
An fling im big ovasize baddy
Pan I young virgin sista,
Tear up har baddy an destroy har mind.
Mek har mad an hate all man.
Mek I young mind revolt gainst de condition.

Yeh. I go a school.
An I pass de sociaty test dem.
An I get a job inna de sociaty institution.
But wah, I still live inna de ghetto.
So even doah I do I work an dem sey I intelligent
Dem still see I as one a de ghetto devil dem.

Yes. Inna de ghetto wey gunman, police an solja
Look de same
From de backside a den gun barrel. KILLER.
Wey I nuh count.
Far police an solja an de res a sociaty
Nuh see I as smaddy.
Dem see I as Savage. Animal. Rapist. Thief. Murderer.
Lazy. Wicked. Hooligan. John Crow. Henchman.
    Gunman.
PNP. JLP. Dutty Bway.

True. I smoke de herb.
But it nuh do I nutten.
But sociaty nuh like it wen it smoke dung yah
So dem vank I.

But wen de uptown sociaty smoke it
Dem canshus.
Seet?

So I go home
To de ghetto
An I look pan de injustice.
I look pan I bredren.
An I nuh decide fi lef
I flesh an blood dung deh.

One day I trod wid I spar
Dung to Forbidden Territory
An true dem mark I sey I come from so
Even doah I nuh a gunman.
I tell my spar sey I haffi proteck I self.
Far dat is de ongle way dat I can stay alive
Inna de ghetto.
But wah,
Dem done check fi I, an set I up fi a fall.

An dem shot I up, Bayonet I. Tek I baddy mek a
           dartboard.

But don' cry madda, don' cry sista, don' cry dawta.
Far doah de baddy inna dis bax well shat up,
I man free.
Free from cruelty. Oppression. Discrimination. Hate.
Inna de ghetto.
But I spirit still siddung pan de gate a tek een de scene.
De cruelty. Oppression. Discrimination. Hate.
Inna de ghetto
An wait.

15

Pamela Mordecai

Mongoose

Poems are shorter; the truth
look — see the mangoose slip into
the bush! quick, after it!
won't stay past these few words

Once the sun moving held earth still
and the stars musical: the swish-
tailed mongoose etherized on his
own breathing slept in a red round.

Dawn and the shiny skin sweat
for the life outside . . . foliage riffled
a new creature sinuated
in: we bought his weave, bit dirt

The animal was out. Time passed
before a certain hunter bayed
him on a tree; no obeah
to beat that down

and now with reason the small
furry thing is off again
mind's rot the wood; its tail
flashing come-ons, we panting

see it always disappear

Poet's World

Poems grow
in window boxes
or especial corners
of kitchens
where rats hide
or offices where men
above the street
desert their cyphers
of the market place
to track the clouds for rain
or ride the wind
guileless as gulls
oblivious of the girl
upon the desk
who proffers wilting breasts
for a fast lunch — Ah which of us
wants anything but love—

and first upon the hillside where bare feet
in a goat's wake avoiding small brown pebbles
know earth as it was made and men in fields
releasing cotton from the mother tree
milking tits heavy with white wholesomeness
or riding wave on wave of green cane till
the swell abates and the warm wind
finds only calm brown surfaces
thick with the juicy flotsam of the storm
make poems

and men who speak the drum
bembe dundun conga dudups cutter
or blow the brass or play the rhumba box
or lick croix-croix, marimba or tack tack
and women who record all this
making the tribe for start in blood
and sending it to school to factory
to sea to office, university   to death
make poems

and we who write them down
make pictures intermittenly
(sweet silhouettes, fine profiles,
a marked face) but the bright light
that makes these darknesses
moves always always beyond mastery
Griot older than time
on Zion hill
weaving a song into eternity.

Revelation *for D.C.*

Yesterday
told me your name
in a place
surrounded
by wind
and hard
bright colours

Late
from his plane
he shook
my hand
mistook me
for your
woman
said
'I am
nice to you
because
your surface
pleases.'

That afternoon
I walked
almost an hour
avoiding dogs
looking
at people
talking
over fences
searching
for eyes

Told
a young man
not to
shoot birds
he said
'It's O.K.—

    I miss
    any way
    my hand
    is lean.'

    Slowly
    the day grew
    I was glad
    to know you

Death Note

Next I shall see your death note
half an inch on a brown page:
at night the cars will drag
their pools of blood behind them still
and I shall know proceeding on the road
stopping and going with the red and green
that it awaits my piece.
I've missed you:
I've wondered if we could have rung
that so bright bell these many many years.
You should know that I drive with confidence—
the road's familiar now;
I'll tell you — every now and then
I dream that I can fly:
somehow I'm certain that
the note brings wings.

Up Tropic *for Martin*

More
than I want

to eat
at your feet

or blow you
bright poems

or winnow
your wheat

with the sieve
of my body

more
than I want

to breed you
bright children

to tickle
your laughter

and tug
at your hair

with
lithe toes

more
God knows

I want
my own greening

So
be it

my black
earth

my water
my air

or free
me up

tropic
for rooting

else
where

Walker 2 *for Grace Walker Gordon*

You blew in
on spirit breath
big, black
well being
danced
to Jesus
choruses
brought
prophecy
and spoke
in tongues

My mean soul
blessed you

You let me talk
listening through
shrill decibells
of who and
why I loved,
when, in what
need, how
well or ill

You listened
listened
heard
as I poured
out the long
libation
word on word
the drizzle of
a little life

You spoke
with caution
gently; ministered
love and discipline
and blessed me
into ministry

So now I bless you
One love in this Wood
One Breath one Body
in His name who heard

it all in the first silence

Protest Poem *for all the brothers*

1. An ache is in a man: towns do not ache,
   nor ghettoes fester; the ravening gnaws
   at bellies, one-one; hurt is personal.
   On the corner, again and again, see
   me sit with my needle and spoon, see me
   puffin' my spliff, see me splittin' my mind,
   see me teenager dead from the blows of
   your words that baptize me according to
   Lenin and Marx — "You are no one, no one."

2. Blessed be the proletariat whom
        we must mobilize
        we must motivate
        we must liberate
        we must educate
        to a new political awareness.

3. Is di ole chattel ting again: di same
   slavery bizness, but dis time di boss
   look more like we an im does be smarter.
   Not a damn soul goin' mobilize my ass
   to rass — dem jokin. Any fool can read
   Das Kapital: what is dat to de poor?

4. We the people propose
        the abolition of you
        and us: we propose
        an acknowledgement
        of our persons and
        an alliance of poverty;

we propose to share the little
that breeds on these
antilles, one mango
to one mouth:

we propose to speak
your language
but not abandon ours;
we insist that you understand
that you do not
understand us.
You may begin
by not shouting —
we are tired of noise.

5. On the corner again and again see
me stand with my pride and my children, my
quiverful, lot, my portion of life; see
me labour and wait; see me plan and scratch
dust for a yam root, a corn, bellyful.

6. See ME
Look!
I am
here
I am
here
I am
here.

Notes on contributors

Jennifer Brown is a radio producer and journalist working with JAMAL. She has had poems published in *Caribbean Quarterly, Arts Review, Jamaica Journal, The Jamaica Daily News, Africa Woman,* and in *The Caribbean Poem,* an anthology edited by Neville Dawes and Anthony McNeill for Carifesta '76.

Christine Craig, currently studying at the University of the West Indies, has worked with the Women's Bureau. *Savacou* and *Arts Review* have published stories and poems by her. Her other publications include radio and television scripts, a film script "Women in Crisis", a family life text for Youth Community Training Centres, and a career booklet for the Women's Bureau. She is the author of two children's books, *Emmanuel Goes to Market* and *Emmanuel and His Parrot,* illustrated by Karl Craig and published by the Oxford University Press.

Jean D'Costa, who was a Senior Lecturer in English at the University of the West Indies, now writes full-time. She does a regular column for *The Sunday Gleaner* on language. The author of three novels for children: *Sprat Morrison* (Ministry of Education, Jamaica), *Escape to Last Man Peak* (Longman), and *Voice in the Wind* (Longman), she is currently at work on a historical novel set in Jamaica in the 1770's, to be published by the Oxford University Press.

Dorothea Edmondson is doing postgraduate work in English. She has written newspaper artices and has had poems published in *The Canadian Forum, East African Journal, Zuba, Pan-African Journal, Water, Jamaica Journal,* and *Arts Review.*

Lorna Goodison is a scriptwriter and artist, currently employed by the Agency for Public Information. She has had poems published in *The Gleaner, The Jamaica Daily News, Jamaica Journal, Savacou, Nimrod,* and in *The Caribbean Poem,* an anthology edited by Neville Dawes and Anthony McNeill for Carifesta '76.

Sally Henzell has written book reviews and done illustrations for *The Gleaner.* Some of her poetry has been published in *Jamaica Journal.*

Bridget Jones is a Senior Lecturer in the Department of French at the University of the West Indies. She has directed plays, and has done film criticism for *The Sunday Gleaner.* Her publications include articles on Orlando Patterson and on Leon Damas.

Sandy McIntosh is Chief Reporter in charge of Features at *The Jamaica Daily News,* and is the recipient of seven Seprod Awards for outstanding journalism. She has written feature articles for various newspapers, and has had short stories and poems published in *The Gleaner, Children's Own, Swing,* and *The Jamaica Daily News.*

Alma Mock Yen is a broadcaster, currently a production assistant at the UWI Institute of Mass Communications. She is the author of *F.Y.I. Your Message Through The Media*, a handbook for laypersons. She has been an actress and a leading dancer. In 1970 she was awarded a bronze Musgrave Medal for choreography by the Institute of Jamaica. She has had poems broadcast by the BBC, and has published short stories and poems in a number of journals and anthologies, including *Public Opinion, The Gleaner, Arts Review, Jamaica Journal* and *Focus*.

Velma Pollard is a Lecturer in Education at the University of the West Indies. Her publications include articles on Edward Brathwaite and on code switching in Jamaica Creole. She has had short stories published in *Jamaica Journal* and poems in *Bim, Arts Review* and *Caribbean Quarterly*.

Heather Royes is currently a Ph.D. student in Mass Communications. A communications specialist, she has been Public Relations Officer for the National Dance Theatre Company since 1970. She has published many feature articles, particularly on Jamaican culture, and has had poems published in the *Jamaica Festival Anthology 1977*, in *Arts Review* and in *BA SHIRU*.

Olive Senior, who was Publications Officer at the UWI Institute of Social and Economic Studies, is now a free-lance writer. She is author of *The Message is Change*, on the 1972 General Elections in Jamaica (Kingston Publishers), and is now writing a book on the West Indians who helped to build the Panama Canal. She has had poems and short stories published in *Jamaica Journal, Savacou,* and *The Caribbean Poem,* an anthology edited by Neville Dawes and Anthony McNeill for Carifesta '76.

Colleen Smith-Brown is a schoolteacher, currently doing a UWI Diploma course in Library Studies with special emphasis on children's libraries. She has had poems published in the *Jamaica Festival Anthology.*

Cyrene Tomlinson is an advertising creative copywriter/ director at McCann Erickson. She is an actress. She has had poems published in *The Jamaica Daily News* and broadcast by the Jamaica Broadcasting Corporation.

Pamela Mordecai is Publications Officer at the UWI School of Education. She used to teach English and has been a radio/tv/film/interviewer/presenter for JIS/ API. She has had poems published in *Bim, Savacou, Jamaica Journal, Arts Review, Caribbean Quarterly, Nimrod,* and in anthologies, *The Caribbean Poem* (edited by Neville Dawes and Anthony McNeill for Carifesta '76), *Ambakaila* and *Parang* (edited by Cecil Gray for Nelson).

Mervyn Morris is a Senior Lecturer in English at the University of the West Indies. He edited *Seven Jamaican Poets,* an anthology (Bolivar Press), and is the author of three books of poems: *The Pond* (New Beacon Books), *On Holy Week* (Sangster's) and *Shadowboxing* (New Beacon Books).

Index of first lines